SPLINTERING SILENCES

Philo Ikonya

Langaa Research & Publishing CIG
Mankon, Bamenda

Publisher:
Langaa RPCIG
Langaa Research & Publishing Common Initiative Group
P.O. Box 902 Mankon
Bamenda
North West Region
Cameroon
Langaagrp@gmail.com
www.langaa-rpcig.net

Distributed in and outside N. America by African Books Collective
orders@africanbookscollective.com
www.africanbookcollective.com

ISBN: 978-9956-791-23-1

© Philo Ikonya 2014

Cover Image by Dr. Helmuth A. Niederle

DISCLAIMER
All views expressed in this publication are those of the author and do not necessarily reflect the views of Langaa RPCIG.

Dedication

My only child Yusufu
I will always love you

About This Collection

Philo Ikonya has published two anthologies: *Out of Prison - Love Songs* (2010 Löcker, Vienna) a bilingual book in German and English and *This Bread of Peace* (2010, Lapwing, Belfast). These are beautifully written powerful poems. They are full of the energy of the poet's insight.

In Splintering Silence, the poet takes us to the source of her strength and power. Her poems rise from a gamut of experiences and thoughts, her philosophy and vision. Poetically, Philo who lives in exile in Norway, explains her journeys. She travels from a rich garden inside her to unravel her ability and versatility. She has her own Alphabet there. She is not confined to any one Geographical space. She cannot be and so the silence splinters in the planets, orbits and a globe that is open to her.

These journeys are physical as such places like Juba in South Sudan, Oslo in Norway and Harare in Zimbabwe inspire her poems published here, but they are also psychological. Three poems: *I count my bones, I count my Children's bones* and *I cannot count his bones* traverse the book and in this last one the activist arises with her answer to greed.

The family is the nation and is compared to it and a society suffering the ills of oppression and humiliation where women and children's bones stick out and can be counted as the men's are covered with soft flesh. No forms of oppression whether from domestic or other imperialistic tendencies are okayed. Polygamy and men who only look after their bellies will not stand in her way.

So many sounds, but the sound of silence is the most powerful. The poet is inspired by the unparalleled song, The

Sound of Silence, by Simon and Garfunkel. She calls it one of the greatest and most mysterious poems of all times. The writer's soul expands and feels compassion in her meditation of the lyrics of that song crafted soon after the shooting of JF Kennedy in 1963.

Philo takes us to those not so prominent who suffer as in the poem *Bow and Pray* which is about the one who bleeds in silence in the poem. She says, silence that makes sense must be probed by the I, by oneself through a daring and loving introspection for change begins with one. But the result must be shared: 'Take my words that I might reach you' and the result is not certain and therefore the agony of the poet.

In this amazing collection, soulful, reflective and introspective the poet searches with us even into her own name. The one she was given by her ancestors and the ones she is called by. She says darkness is visible in light but both are us and therefore we must reach for the 'I' and surprise ourselves hailing yourself: *Hello Darkness My Old Friend!*

This book is a celebration of the resilience of spirit and a constant loving compassion for the love of humanity. The poet connects with activism and change in practical ways and liberating thoughts.

Table of Contents

Splinters 1
Light 3
Sound 6
Traversing 8
Pledge 11
Striving 14
Exile 16
You 19
Wake Oslo up again 21
Dafuri huts by Akerselva 23
Storm that touches sound 25
My Name 28
Hovering 34

Sparks 37
The Split 39
Samosa 40
The Nile in Juba 41
Arm 44
Cobblestones 47
Bow and pray now 49
I count my child's ribs 51
Labour pains for a continent 53
Places in us 55
Sounds voices share 56
Here and there 58
Silent sound dance 59
Oslo for once wriggles in heat 60
Rich ways 62
Juba-man-o'-war 65

Mother.. 69

Flying.. **71**
Word... 73
Flight.. 74
If I could... 76
Leaving Juba... 79
Diplomatic happy hour.. 81
Sunrise for Roma.. 84
I count my ribs... 86
Allah Akhbar... 88
Beauty.. 90
High.. 91
Stereo plays... 92
Wash me.. 94

Rage..**97**
So betrayed... 99
Fresh..103
Never seen my body.. 104
Gu'nai.. 105
Refuge...107
A Saturday sunrise...109
Christiania home... 112
Nautical smiles.. 114
Nairobi soils...116
Bouquet.. 118
Morning unfolds for some......................................121
I cannot count his ribs.. 123
Fragrances..128
Warrant of arrest... 129

SPLINTERS

Light

Blind I have come from far
Never fared this way before
I delight in my garden
of alphabets much older than Eden
Only energy within is left
in this paradise not lost
for here my host is my guest
we can communicate

Something sits in these alphabets
that I break alone in lit simplicity
This is dough that we must eat
without fear everywhere
Break silence and
greet darkness your old friend
What the Garden of Eden told Olduvai
Sing!

Look at the woods now
They are climbing the mountains
They laugh as waters there swim
racing down and rising
Grasses grow echoing the reeds
lilting they are singing
Dust becomes life
spreading, writing, reading
Unknown new seeds are
printing on stems of papyrus
to keep memory lush

I find my way for we speak
to break
The smithereens shine and
we heal our wounds with
salve salivated greetings
to repair we speak
To live we speak to love
For all the forgotten aves
that flew away
I bow

In between splutters of silence
give more meaning to sound
than words that slim in thought
tread in dry throats
and cry kill
Everywhere bandaged
they hide the light
of living letters
in prism penetrating hearts
Colour
Remaining sweetness unending
light unbending forever clear
Snakes syrupy visible in darkness
like cat eyes harmless and settled
Innocent lions suckling oryx and
baby baboons daily tick picked

A flash of darkness in the light
is the lamp that lights our gorge
In this mildewed orchard lichen
our pen is in naked light

Here where words grow green
so gently we wear no leaves
Multiply and increase
Even divided you still fructify
Enlightening to darken and darkening
to enlighten
the troubadours
of night
light

Sound

Sowing many stories never tires
the soul ekes broken silences and
sounds that pray like calabashes
holding dry seeds of creeds
that weep into words of gold
singing at sunrise
rays are prayer

In the evening moon song each day
But the smiles on the ground
are covered with miles of thorns
And yet I sweat not nor bleed
before the garden I was heat
in infinity
burning where water refreshed
my soul

Birds will sing and sing and
sounds warble from a stream
My spirit flows unhindered and
spreads hugging dreams
of my skin
my beads dance peace
on my shrubbery gown

Hear the echo of those bangs again
In the ear you inherited Big Bang
All your movements sound again to gain
and again to pleasure and pain release
I wish the word did not split

or did so in silence bursting
into music
but that sounds present past
now future

My garden grows odd philosophical fruits
I have to perch on a branch that
knows her roots and shoot back where
I come from
For before time began perhaps we were
all arrows of speed with noise
aimed at love and flying waves unseen

Dangerous with rage and red poison tipped
pen dancing sperms in handwriting
attracted to the eternal present
always embracing tight
and hugging alphabets
of light
Drilling them into rocks
lips, books, dreadlocks, lands and
planets without end
breaking them into alphamusical
notes again for meaning

Traversing

But now am here after
many ills and hills
Still in my garden
my sunrise is a word
song melts into beats
and hitting rhythms in the sky
are stolen by angels high above my lips
Am well enough in my planet-womb

I was here before I was born
I dreamed light and sound through
And in my mind so many passions honeying
No borders no traces of races without humanity
No passports and visas only love filled here-ness
Bringing garlands for a million halos in Rwanda
Yet still continents afar
bloodying in silence and sound
awake me
turning borders into wreaths musical
for the dead like in Tarantella
Do you remember a thing?

I am here
I am here in mind land unlocked in woman ways
Flowering like petals heart field ascending
Walking and swimming and
descending in flight
on the wings of breaking words that are universes
I search beneath the seas of words I love
and skies above

        transcend
      mountains of thought and
    music the barrage none can bar

I hug split harmony like stars and planets in orbits
I am the firmament that holds those bodies up high not
        falling
and there, there, who shall we beg for fair hearing
        and air
      into our lungs?
Breathe! Take and eat: This is a mine of justice

Each prophet brings terror*ed* peace to Earth
All proclaim these are God's own editions
One, two and three books always many
No lingua franca of peace outside space in words

Crush and harvest my words until they explode
like pods in the sun bursting to flight again and heal
Squeeze out meaning and dance the sound of silence
till pain ultimately irrigates those agitated dreams again
      in meditation

    I rise and traverse
Let my words like splintered silence
fall and echo and drop into a reservoir of whispers of pain
and ask, who can stay still in restlessness?

Run in the rain
in a deluge create all languages of signs and punch racism
beat your drum on the piano and breaking into Noah's Ark
    find a philia harmonica in hip hop too

with no limits to rhythm and song
traverse but sing
Hello darkness my old friend!
Sing traditional, merge and form
and break and eat and
sing again in the poets home
Oyaiii, Oyaiii
Traversing
sing away
and sway

Pledge

I tore my way
from home for freedom, and free
Yet need so many bonds that truly bind
like a child to a mother and her country
And so many, many minds
I plead to unite in this one land
beginning with a weary breast

That rain falls everywhere
not choosing domains I cannot contest
it follows thunder in the wake of lightning
Only oftentimes it pours all the time on one
blinding recovered light deafening
Hear those claps as if that is not enough proof
why are hearts planted in blood - group coding
and what has pigmentation to do with it all?
In Europe you wince that is why am in exile
My sisters are nomads eternally disowned

At home
You will remind me
that I am only free on a legal bond
bailed out like they told me
in Harare 2008
and in faith retell me
am neither Peter, Paul or James
only Gasheri in bonds
and writing letters to more
than the Hebrews

I tell you to sleep well
I merged with freedom
long before you broke on me the law
The sky opens and cracks its stars to light

I have flown my wings of freedom
My heart of longing tucked well in my chest
I have long known that
I connect with many thoughts in you
for whom they are one
that I see who
I really am
Votes I have in plenty
power ringing like ancient Indian said
'Tread softly in Spring the earth is pregnant'
I give birth in pain alone
and there is an aura around the sun

When I witness Afrika
You tell me come back home
global concerns drive people mad
Here near the fire you have uhuru
cold and damp are shut out
But for shouting: Down, corruption down!
Out of handcuffs am jeered
and again am out on bond
Do you wish I united with rot?

Should I shout out corruption where all dies
in the slums and
At the feet of the Dalai Lama
beg China for

anti-corruption prayers?

I have turned my skirt into a huge
house of imagination
imaging nations
You can have my rough cloth top
and everything else
I wear my skin and bones
I am a sackcloth soul of hope
in the boundless torture
of hard ropes
I learn

*uhuru, Kiswahili for freedom

Striving

The people died singing
and not one poem was published
and their tongues
were left folded frolicking in ulalations
which I change from *aririririiriii*
to *Friiiiririiiiriiiiii Friiiiiii Friii,* free
Nothing was posted on Fb and Tweets there were banned
they evaded South Sudan forever
At least vultures make a noise for cadavers
My songs are still locked in tears
I was out again on in South Sudan
with a broken right arm my fork for work
only to feel and more pain to see
Isn't black Africa still in slavery- bound cries my heart?
Africa, did you say?
I want to
archive our brave phrases
of how rich we are
how happy
for no one needs misery spices
the first dimension reported anywhere
I knew bliss playing constantly on my childhood rays of the
sun
but now
There is blood in my basket and the strings wet and rotting
My thrill is perishable at sell-by dates
it comes carrying chocking tears this *arириririiriiii*
Sometimes it is printed on cakes at presidential weddings
baked without national black flour
and no difference wintry season or sizzling Christmas

Alleluias of icing cold
all year round
in roasting heat

Then again in Juba back
my neighbour is a Darfuri and a kaburi is in our chests
a cemetery
old as war and extensive
Reporters are tired
And people dead before their time
throw their rubbish of Rest In Peace
out of pots they return to cook with
flowers
And trees, I see none
Rubbish on graves is in heaps not flowers
I fear I will gray in a minute
of 2009 on this beach so bleak I walk alone
We rest in breach who reaches peace?

Exile

I laugh the distance away
and the sad tears that
want to web my imagination in silence
killing many nations in mine, I feel the pain
I turn my collar again and I hear that sound
I blow in the dark and again in the dark
Greetings darkness our ancient friend, hello!

I dance with light I begin a nation
Finding no positive darkness echoes
I still dare open the promise
Creation is not a notion but inspiration
look how real
I am lord of this dance like a ray
it lasts eternal
When I took light in my eyes and broke it
an image was made to console me
Even without light I would be full of color
who knows what hides in darkness
I laugh the distance away my hope still remains

Amazed I breathe my moments
deeply inhaled like philosophical tea

The moment here is in me
Tomorrow is borrowed and
in today's memory yesterday is buried
but not you, rising and falling
You are
You live in the well of silence

my land, our hero
You are alive
Resurrection has no borders
You are back
I love the sound of your laughter
Your playful eyes informed and full
Always breaking rays of light and reflecting
Seeing me and the other and all of us there
The way you give birth to me dispels gloom
of ethnicism divisive

See how we fill our eyes and laugh in there
and our laughter is not mini like the pupil
We expand and laugh and live and grow so magical
We are warm and happy and light in sorrow

And the distance has faded away
If you believe in dying forever
Who will measure the absence?

Now in moments we hold hands
and look at the instance of silence
We are all in this other exile
yet we must still be lords
of this dance too
Goodnight JM Kariuki, goodnight
I shatter the exile of the
bullets of the assassins with
this song of hope for you
for your child
and grandchild
Kenya

*JM Kariuki visionary politician assassinated in Kenya on March 2 1975

You

This other splintering
silence
silence, ilence, lence, nce, sss
aches
You do not smile
You do not sing
You do not dance
You do not write
You do not talk
You do not laugh
You do not eat
You do not read
You do not hold a speech
sit in the sitting room or
push the clutch to our graduations
You do not phone
You do not get sick
You do not drink
You do not complain
You do not make love
You do not pray
You do not return
My Father
You do not breathe

Even when the village path is hungry
hungry for your feet entry free
at Tom Mboya Hall
You do not open those eyes
Once so wide like lights burning

You are gone

I know no other rift so deep
my journey became so long
I tell you about it with love
but it includes the word exile
and you were a detainee for freedom
Were we not both to say
Good morning Freedom?
This night is so long

Wake Oslo up again

At first I thought the sun would never come
but it left the cloud above, now pale blue
and came down painting buildings
not minding its icy ways
I do not know why it avoided the church spire
perhaps it was too high to inspire

We saw long clothes, we failed to see him
Watching his youthful eyes and eagerness
we missed the dashing spark in his iris
the cold that said he was looking for recognition
dying to be hugged on earth and in heaven

We did not see his brain was a computer
Cold calculus huge math in -patient blows
longing to be touched and loved in service
force of creativity new barriers breaking
The violent light of a bomb awakens us
invisible white its smoke
But the light of the sun
has kissed everything underneath
flower seeds stir a little
the walls of our flats where faith might be
begin to warm up
I look and still

The black lamp hanging on your balcony
the white crow again as the sparrow flies
returning in a group to do three journeys
to the power of three so many victories

Soon I will see the ground heat up
for the sun rays caress the ground
Soon I will see the flowers hold up again
and the song of hope will go on forever
Soon I will see the dust rise again
and even if it be deep winter on sudden night
I will take off my shoes
and bring him home to warmth

*Written in Oslo before the bomb of July 2011

Dafuri huts by Akerselva

Africa is here in many silhouettes
This is Oslo's listening day
This man of Sudan cries in tongues
about:
Darfur. Darfur. Darfur
Dafuri
and his lost African language
The Janjaweed growing on his chest and
always in his nightmares he walks alone
Shabaabs in Somalia so many jabs
Bashir and Khartoum and Dafuris
Salva Kiir and Jongolei, what of Juba?

Mogadishu is pregnant with Nairobi
Eastleigh trembled till he left but he smiles
at the memory of the Section One, Section Two, Three
and Eight and then 16th Street now so far away
Poor man is thin but his head so full his skin weeps

He retreats in deep thought to the Indian Ocean
Mombasa yells and he too
at Fort Jesus' invisible disunity
He draws home in Darfur
on the banks of Akerselva
in deep fear frustration
I listen in pain as the water flows he says
My Mother died, my Father, my wife, my…my
my… my… my… my… my…died, my friends
died. My…
Aiii

All souls unique half a million dead and
two million and more homeless whom
shall he talk to again?
He names Bashir again
He scratches the ground with sticks
and draws round country maps like huts
He holds his heart for long
Then
Out of the reeds he takes
a prayer mat and leaves to meet
his brothers in the mosque
He has given peace to himself
in his circles, he has given it to us in huts
in cities of the world away from home -
I am lost in word
thought
and deed
And the Janjaweed are still increasing in silence today
At home I flow on Television
but cannot see
My eyes pierced by light now will darkness heal?
Commemoration of Rwandese Genocide twenty years ago
this machete is still alive and smoking
I want to birth new lands
Millions anti-genocide we have to decide
to care
Dare recreate words in a new alphabet of justice
that disturbs the sound of silence
this night and
forever more

Storm touches sound

Sometimes the shores are quiet and
life sweeps back and forth in waves
beneath the corona moonlight shivers
I feel like they touch our arteries kissing
when small waters are playing with the shores
Moving as if in a dance of pebbles
Stones play big mountains
the waters little hide and seek
as if there were no sea dangers out there
but the rocks are under and over you too,
silent arms in deep restless water
Your ear fans the water *siririririririiririri!*

When you swim and the waters court your ear
Other waters are that do not care
They bash Simon and Sithole's boats
Ships they wrecked before and scattered
the debris all around Robben Island- humans
Sriiii riiiii riiiiii riiiiiii riiiiiii riiiiii listen fools
Have you been to Lampedusa black and blinded?
Watching for dawn as the horizon is broken?

And yet the way of the heart must live
love so burning for you does not bury resistance
as we keep eating fish that eat us in seas 'terranean
See so many others still swirl in the sea
singing songs that writers never hear
Try to keep your voice afloat on dry land
Try to find where her palm still strokes so you know
to caress the bald head of the earth covered with water

to calm rough tides and keep our oars moving
It is dangerous to keep still, search for peace to make love
shriiiiiiiiiiiiiiiiiiiiiiiisriiiiiiiiiisriiiiiiiiiiiiiiiiiisriiii
Search for peace, reach me and reach us

A huge storm comes from elsewhere
bursting on a tiny phone left in a tent seething
news of a bomb on land and over ferry
another on the Outer Island, Utøya
a massacre echoes in the sound of blood
Uolololo! uolololololo! Mola!Uolololo!
Storm of news that smashes our universe
Shrikrukishkreeekbangheee,iiiii,aaahhSkkjjggg
åååååååååååååååååååååååååååååååååååbangååååååååh
in a little gadget just hanging around there new words
breaking the silence of the quiet coast with pain

Debris returns to Isle de Goree, Robben Island
Rubble to Rome and Kismayu
rumble now or be quiet
There are many histories
prisoner consciences don't sing
Over there not over still
Viking ways still lurk

They do not sing at Rangoon
they are Ruhingya
Not in the Indian Ocean where pirates
dive and change into thieves
So when shall all human islands
show in us the divine?
And out there ring *freee, freee, freee eeeiaa weee!*

What warning flashes here
what sign do words write?

Sriiii lalallaalaaaa! Sriiiiii lalalalaaaa!
Sriiiiiiiiiilalala!
Breaking so many silences
like waters foaming and playing
the shores of humanity's toes moving as if prophets are writing
in a dance of waters so calm to round all islands
writing on walls of water on both sides of a path cleared by God
Was that not enough for an image before tenement halls?
Sriiii lalallaalaaaa! Sriiiiii lalalalaaaa! Sriiiiiiiiiilalala!
Can you hear without listening?
Can you tell without moving tongue?

My Name

Philo = Love
Who would such a laurel deny?
If I should take mine now
and spread it out on a globe
would it be thick in the middle
and below even thicker
and at the top enough to write Philo
for Love in fullness of meaning
crowning?
All over a globe of justice
touching seas and mountains
or would it be lost in one little cave endless like
splintering silences of the name
they gave me at birth and a tongue
they spoke to me at to be born?

Can now my names hold all borders
covering the outer layers of stone
or deep creeks enough for little
and big fish to swim:
Omena, pirhana, bagigi so many—
with sharks and dolphins and whales?

How shall a woman play naked light
When she has no place to stand
Should she break into the great mind the hut of Sophia
and smash the pot of
wisdom
She should delete all non-proverbs forever in this one:
'Women are the source of all evil it is only our souls that have saved us'

a non-verb Oh Afrika!
Two feet on a piece of land without ground
Voice comes from between bone marrow
Tell the soft ones am coming to talk to you again
After I cross the endless seas
in the narrow corridors of power
Walking on a name that is only greeted
by those who dare
Name my ancestors blessed unto me
after whispering soft sounds
to the four winds and crying out
more vision sighting without fear
Name no one wrote on paper
'Alillilliiriiiii frrriii Njeri She has come

I am living now on added holy names
language vulgarized reclaiming
my alphabets in this gold mine
of a garden of all time

My names both new and traditional
sliced
mean who loves in
heart and hears words
adores too in movement
and like all of us wakes up to fish hope

I had options if the spirit would agree
but it said no
No to Wa Njia, child of the road
the visitor's path is not paved
To a barren woman

tongues are so unkind
that my aunt held my womb
to heal hers unconceiving
Borrowed mine younger and waiting
for my own children for her glory
She gave herself and to me grace in the name of love
to reproduce our ancestors
She never looked back
in the name of love
grace

Her work became life
wisdom that swirls while moving
must clear the ground and sculpt power out of air
staying to live and alive
like a monument of breath that visits your eyes
with life and delight into your lungs
I grow and come again to ask
where the burning lamp is
for surprise incarnation
You did not expect me
such power in word
under a bed?

Mother would also confirmation give me
Elizabeth´s old fertility subtle connections
The priest was blind I had to be the cousin
conceiving in old age
testifying to this I ask
was Hannah not enough?
Anna must be hidden
in my passport too?

I am not a name
just call me woman
Love that crushes and breaks traditions

What does Anna mean in your Mother Tongue?
Must I reject my own garden of alphabets to be me?
Are we here more than orphans so bereaved of sounds
that we hang sentences like necklaces on our necks
new chains of letters meaning none?

I have to make meaning now for peace to grow with all
ancestors
round this planet earth where we must speak to animals and
plants
If we really long for peace
All things around us
must be caressed and loved for bombs not to explode
Hiroshima unforgotten has
multiplied over and over again
feeding grenades in Somalia
If I am Anna I must fly
to tell you that
You fail the test too often
Woman is

Anna is eagle in man but woman
flies higher in all of them
Full of grace and favor we share one skirt of blood
In Sanskrit Anna is a grain to sprout
like love unplanted
it grows and I no longer walk alone
for the people to bow and pray

See how I spread me on my globe
till it wipes Hannah's tears
and soon floats Musa along a river
again
straight into my breast to suckle

I open the passing rivers and write
My name is love, my name is Love
I am Love
I have thrown my desire to be safely
home with dissident affection
down streams of dreams
writing gently on reeds and reading
every tongue
In Japanese I learn Anna is an apricot
so from Nara and take the sign and read
Eat my love
I return to root

See how the base of my tree widens
I spread these roots so
no planet disappears in the universes
for there is not only one
but many

I rename my planets one by one
I have your mind captive now
'United many spiders can tie a lion'
Ethiopian proverb
What can fail us in sounds of languages
when there is no 'if' anymore?

Why then would everything not meet the eye?
It is all in ancient light that sees so far
My Venus is Issis, my sun Achieng
and moon Wambui mother colonized by Mumbi
claiming creation of everything forgetting Kit Mikayi
Must Chelegat and Amirah be Mars bleeding?
When you return
I will give you my breasts
Dialogue must survive if this is democratic
and we must not leave out Naliaka, Daisy
Heidi and Lorena women of different Geography
our continent is named concern

Hovering

Hovering like words written on the air
of a room long ago occupied
loved in to be lived in
by thoughts so tender in memory
Glowing notes of music
growing like tendrils wall to wall
The music you play is weaving me
Your fingers and eyes careful
To search the note of the moment
Piped from room to room, alive
I stay in each note and give soul and spirit
Body is nothing without them
Oneness sharing without breaking
into two and three to lose the one

For we dance and our legs become one
We move and our hands become body
We breathe and the air fills muscle with
Beauty and energy, the warmth of life in lips
Silence
Then I hear you say something
about listening to silences-
Am mute
Now subtlety tells me to say no more
You went to live in the time full of stars
Nobody knows, none can tell, none can see
Or answer why sleep is part of that departure
And silence a mine is filled with meaning
And tears, waters that gently fill
Explode, exploring and imploring my soul and run

down to my lips over mouth tasting
of salt preserver of being
tears
roll to my chin untouched
Reach the room of silence in me
Love in, Live in
Drip down, in drops so long, so long
My heart is drinking you and the tears
in my heart to a savory
Amen

SPARKS

The split

Have you felt the pain of the sword
that drives between you and your loved one?
Have you felt how in racism, it drives recklessly
between your skin and blood, the cells and hair and
how it makes the others' eyes old?
Have you felt it colder than ice
cutting deeper than a machete?

Have you felt how the knife cut
between you and your sister, your brothers
become strangers, have you felt this?
Have you felt the knife try
to cut your teeth to the gum
to slice your bones to blood?

Have you heard shrapnel
raining on every home you know
and the news is that you have been bombed
by a powerful nation because your people do
not surrender
have you?
Have you then seen your people surrender to drugs
to poverty of loss and gain
the search for nirvana
blow out?

Samosa

These are three sides triangular
hidden power in the middle
Rip one side, bite and sip all
Power in three needs movement
Splinters
flying
sparks

I have seen the ancient star
and the oldest woman on earth
at all times still smiling
telling stories to the rivers
To a man of toothless gum

If I lost my tears in hers
I will find them in the sea
white like pearls now my earrings
richness you never imagined
black beauty the filling in a pyramid

The Nile in Juba

Is it true that as I sailed and surfed
on internet beside you
Your waters decidedly sluggish
and so eternally calm
you were sending a million messages to the stars
for Africa's *Halley's comet to come

Is it true that I have just missed Cleopatra's barge
Africa still blowing trumpets
for empires rolling drums
Is this it?

That hiding
in you are crocodile -hard cover volumes
silent unopened
longing to be read
hiding metaphysics in Mother Tongue dancing?

And that
long, long stories
are swimming in a waterproof
world library
in the internet
flowing
floating past every poet's
hut
our great stories
bidding the entire world listen?

All weekend, both men and women

children
will swim naked in you
drink you and smile you
because in this land
without sprays of water
on soft and hard cover monuments
starlight fades everywhere
Is it true?

We delight in you on the nights when you post
high figures in Cairo
and you remember your mother Lake Victoria our Sango
Flood in before our continental boat is pirated
before never reaching Tanzania wrecked
your waves must rock our basket

Sometimes I dream I comb your delta head
your hair flying
I toss you up in the air
like a childgod Musa* playfully enchanted
swimming busily in your reeds
We are for love and laughing
and then I fling you out!
You water all our dry Nubia*
Our Africa
Our Nilo

---

* Halley's comet can be seen with the naked eye. Writer saw it in 1986. It comes every 76 years and is associated with luck for some and failure for others. The comet's appearance in 1066 was recorded on the Bayeux Tapestry. In 1066, the comet was seen in England. Later that year Harold II of England died in the Battle of Hastings. For William the Conqueror it was a good omen. The comet is seen as a fiery star, and the surviving accounts describe it as appearing to be four times the size of Venus, with three times the light of the moon. It is expected back in 2061.

** Musa is Moses in Kiswahili and other languages. Biblical Moses's being hidden in the reeds is evoked.

*** Nubia is a region of southern Egypt and northern Sudan. Is it also an old civilization.

Arm

When I return to our village
holding an I Pad
with the arm you broke older but healed
Will the air there be fresh and green?
Will the fields be fresh or dying gold?
Will the wheat be holding its sheaf and
the maize be decking burning brown
or honey-dark strands so lovely blacking?
Will it be fair to shoot you endlessly for pics?

When we return to my village

Will there still be a lone shepherd
counting his sheep and singing to cows
and a shepherd girl in a long torn skirt
holding a stick that she jumps above
sometimes?

Will anybody know me because they knew my father?
Will there be old women who pronounce his name
with a flutter of heart's beating without him
sunset's warmth gone?
Will old men look up and laugh with starts and stops
and then clear their throats peeping to the heavens
a finger to gently silenced lips?

Will anyone remember chalk
on my mother's hands
her smile celebrate like one day
when they told me her fairy tale ways

a wedding day of shared seats of the car?
Will the old man Joeku who laughs
calling out "One Day!" the nickname they
gave one another still cry of joy and
flying crow's feet flee from
the corners of his eyes with the salt of
his tears?
Will he stare at my face and
take my arm for long
before speaking again?
When I return
will the rains be peeping from above
or rudely flooding all soils made into one cake
Shall we rise to meet the dust or shall we be of it part?
Will there be little chats in front and behind
when we turn and see people coming and going
in gesticulations?

Will I find you?
Will I find you still reading a book
like Chief Albert Luthuli
the great teacher
at the porch of the house
where evening rays sing hope to pages
and lullabies to sleep as you caress their ears?

I yearn to meet you
will I?
I must find you for whom
my heart so longs and sings songs
books in crook I brook
silent communion so strong

because in the wings of my dreams
I must find you
in
myself
and see you in
my arm

Cobblestones

In the wedding of the elements
I gathered clean vines and
wreathed wonders
kiss earth water kiss earth
Earth sip and sip and sip
Sun burn up water burn out
Life is moving, moving up
Rain is falling, falling up
Down is up and up is down
Have you seen the sky in a puddle?
Lightning is a shadow now
It is raining
who knows what?
It is raining we see water
Inside water is a hungry moon
and voices angelic sing inside the rain

It is raining musically
Stars searching for more love
melted like angry god clouds
The trembling soul of rain weeping
begs me to feel the pain of earth ceasing
Like a child made with pleasure
and painful contractions caressing
No killer floods ladder to earth
to leave us homeless when earth kiss sky
and water sows fertility in embrace
Life moving up and down
when down is heaven and
up this sky its twin

Kiss earth water kiss earth
for life the air flies by
The fragrances of a hundred bushes rise in me
Strength that nobody can steal again
It is raining wisdom, power and joy
It is raining really raining
In my mind
in my
heart and soul

Bow and pray now

Deep within and
steeped in silence
submerged in my amazing underworld
of no words, just I, esse undivided
everything tells its story silently
And I see, I hear, I see, I hear, I see
that you have not been here
Where music is a place that questions
judges and heals even fools
I see you always on TV first

Your face is wrinkled by greed
Your sweat has no salt but poison
Your skin is unvisited by gentleness
That tongue is wagging red
and speaks of war soft or loud
no matter

So much gunfire in politics
In which word can I find
a silent deed of innocence?
Is it between two shells opening
or two sheets a silent bed
with all my pains pretended pleasure?

See

She is bleeding silence
I cannot bear her stillness
those wide open dead eyes there

they speak so loudly to me
She lies still and ever mute
I cannot stand her silent yell now
It cuts me deeper than all words
She sees her world unchanging

Now see her spirit a distant bleeding star
Maybe you will come closer one day
And stroke her essential ways and see
And listen to silence in speech and
hear her pain in conversations on the street
coiled around small village paths unspoken

Growing on forget-me-nots that
fill your old trousers and that
creeping green around her skirt
Talk to me now before nettles blossom
in your throat, silence like stinging nettles

Now bow and pray, bow and pray now
No adoration can be forced
Make no more neon gods
She is here
before you
silent bleeding silence
This is a warning to you forever
The sign that appears out of her
every moon
How have you treated your women gods?

I count my child's ribs

These fingers of mine have
counted the ribs of my son
caressing him on my thigh
and they remember these knuckles
on his hind only back bones

Rub my femur that shakes
my tibia and fibula tremble
I know that there is no knee to cap
my fears
as I verse on vertabrae

I went to school
but I have here certified misery
everyone catches the virus

I have felt the knots in my son's back
This meditation opens my cranium
to a still place

Bones dry and covered black
It was white ones that began to crack
My bones are in my son's
and they are silent as I count them again
we starve for lack of vitamin values
free ways on highways

Every time you tell me there might be a cure
For you it is only the news, breaking news
my sinews are gone

When I count my daughter's ribs
they are broken like mine in her childhood
and I cannot lend her calcium and soul
Who can?
Who will do the next generation's
census of skeletons and souls?

Labour pains for a continent

Juba invited me to bake on her streets
and salt my bread with tears
as huts demolished flew by
like big untidy parasols upside down
the wind sweeps what it can
children try to fly the wings of flies
The cool highlands of Nairobi
I hear calling me but I must ritual yet

My happy news
I bond this land and color
I bond with our deeds for freedom
an ordinary hungry peoples' movement
revolution for you
call it renaissance
I will bond
like contact super glue
I will bond
From ocean to ocean with wings of freedom
I will bond

Bond I will not with uniform and boots
No, not with your guns
Only with Sudan
Afrika free
For justice is peace
Zim on the brim of just justice.
Spreading all over Somalia
being Kenya *damu**
could I be your shield?

My heart is yearning, speaks everything
The president should have been younger and woman
to feel like me labour pains of a continent
I have to flee, I scream till hoarse
I shatter prison walls of Ethiopia
but they rise again stronger embryonic Eritreanic
in Egypt we are all strangers
to freedom since Pharaonic ways
Pyramids are firmly shut
Issis replaced and imprisoned
I cross from sea to sea
your warrant of arrest hits the snow hard
and is iced for your afternoon tea
Our shield and defender is broken
in injustice
Am sorry comrade
I have to find mine in my flight
instead of washing the feet
of your newly born daughter
on welcoming earth
we are alien
Alien
where darkness begins at lunch time for a season
and then Norwegian summer days no night all light
I know what is coming in our endless day
for now still traveling on empty air
I am here free
My feet are searching you
I shall return
and with hope of sanity

*Kenya damu phrase heard often in Kenya, means am Kenyan through and through

Places in us

Sounds are more than we can hear
Sounds are there we cannot hear
There are so many places inside your body
Planets, oceans, stars, hills, plants in shape
railway road wheeled legs
spiral staircases in backbone and ribcage
Waterfalls lianas, balls and walls
guts exhaust pipes tagged
I wish you could kill all tags
stereotypes, yes, kill intestinal
fatal thinking or keep distant like cesspit
grandfathered renew

The depth of silence without measure
We have not seen so many eyes
Looking at us so deep
giraffe and snails
different ways, sounds and ears

Eye like a screen without paint colorful
So many different misty eyeshades
Sight without vision sometimes
But always water to mix the colors
Colors that hear sounds
and taste their taste

Sounds voices share

Hingũrĩraa haaiya hingũrĩraa
Hingũrĩraa, Darling hingũrĩraa
Hingũrĩraa darii hingũrĩraa

In the depth of water mind races past
Vision blossoms when you are sleeping
Where shall I find my own tongue gaining
One stroke after another to take me home
When will molecule whisper to molecule
Or air clasp particle as I tear through to home
Home and singing, Mama am here!
Home and singing Mama am here!
Hingũrĩraũ, Mami hingũrĩraa!

Marriage negotiations are for life
World of proposing without end
Wedding always starting
and never ending
heart marries without ceremony
and eats what it loves ceaseless
would you truly marry me on a time and date
just to kill doubts of humanity?
I am swimming for miles and lost at sea
To be home, to be home, home and still in word
Standing up now I surf flying high
a birr through water continuous sonorous silence
I have now arrived no matter home and loved received
home and hugging children that turn to me
from that far corner some look
at me, run away and come back to me

as I sing:
Hingũrĩraũ, Motherland, hingũrĩraa!
All faces and arms are here
they smile and break into small volcanic joys
We find a new alphabets in immediate photo shoots

Exile gives soul spiritual insight
so they feel your strength irresistible
I am home and stepping on soils I know
Threadbare in ways easy to see
I am standing on land with coastal gifts once taken
for granted before I was grounded by ice
in a sea of endless papers and borders inside passports
Today not tied in chains of unchanging mountains serrated brow
I have known snow edges crumbling, jumped in deep indeed
then walked away on a silent horizons free
Swam in the depth of water melting fast in history
mind races past and returns to body and soul needs
When will I seal
my Love?
Hingũrĩraũ, Mwendwa, hingũrĩraa!

Here and there

It is silent
you are not talking
It is silent
there is no music
It is silent
You are not smiling
It is silent
There is no joy
It is silent
where are the crickets?
It is silent
Where are youth driven cars?
It is silent
There are no smiles
The silence is stretching out over miles

It is silent without the sun
At home it cackles as the hens peck
and it sings all day with cockrels to mark time!
Ask the donkey for a refrain
Sun sings in dry banana fibre *kuruuurrr*
and ripens tomatoes noisily smiling!

Silent Sound Dance

Silence is not always silent
There is a dance to it
in this town, this beat
Not always beautiful
too black to make sense
who cares?
No voices
swish in this and that direction
It is a silence trap
They come quietly
if they laugh I should look down
but not stare at the dog's collar

The sun is out
and worms are hiding
under shades of trees in parks
And here on pavement hot
am out and bold and visible
Not turning skin inside out
with chemical to flirt you
My black skin feels great
and at last from the South
Granny Vitamin D
has come visiting
her tender hands to
caress me and now
You need her too

Oslo for once wriggles in heat

I have never
seen a mirage here
Desert sands are far
I hear them crying
in Lampedusa
it is not so far away
echoes under the sea are forever

In this city here there are many
silent sounds that go cock a cock
but they only talk of
prostitute black girls
where Afrika is a country
what does it matter if they say Nigeria?

Look---

That man is dancing round
and round a cigarette on the ground
after a while he dances down
to a butt
A full bottom is his anchor
Others come and dance
round this maypole
for hours and hours of hours
outside the Ark of books
no flood

He is in the same spot at Brugata sorrow
a sparrow calls him chicken of white and black wings

a hurricane of drugs blows in him today
he cannot pick his imaginary world up
He attempts to pick silent sounds
and raise them up to the sun

They cannot rise up
He swings again and again
for hours
Noah's flood returns
it does in doses here and they say skin is
robbed by drugs underneath
And the sound is gone with a tweet
dancing on air
Some say it is just a summer dance

In winter he would do the same
jump around a stub and a butt
dying in the snow for summer's return
just a dream in a silent choir
Trying to pick up lonely sounds
this silence
watches still

Rich ways

It happened in the last days
of the Roman Empire
Here in Oslo it goes on daily
No empire is going to fall
only snow and more snow
Wash it and it will not become whiter
Strange looks if you forget and ask
if something else is about to fall

Black folk carried burdens
Who was Simon of Cyrene
not to fall under the cross?
Had he no choice but to snigger?
Why, there is something here in name
and word dying -
lying
Dare you ask Theo questions
are you strong enough for his answers?

In this city
satiated they eat and drink
Throwing up is norm
tomorrow there will be more
While rainbow and all folks with forks
eat yolks
worms are hiding underground
and the train speeds by hour after hour
But if you insist -

This is none of your business

There is no underclass here
We have equality here you know –
Like? *Likestilling*, like social equality
Never ever such a thing
as racism
Stilled and distilled
like bottles of mountain water
we sit back complacent waiting to
be drunk
They choose beer and
hear not
Roma singing like all of us
dancing like Afrika
flutes and sounds sound like humanity
travelling all over and getting babies too
Stop it ghettonising facts!
Speak not into the mouth of
freedom of expression!
Ikke snakke i munn!

Deep in the Mediterranean you have enough
to do that maybe in Arabic
Black pen black ink that is how it should be
black words
that in your home people starve
die from hunger
None of your business
if we throw up on our white shoes

I have been many places
and I must fly beyond color
where it snows white I hear

You are too dark
to lead, to sing in the
sound of silence
and so I burst out :-

Hello Darkness My Old Friend!

No!
Play your drum
don't you know?

Oyaaaiii mshairi alimunyumba
mshairi alimunyumba
Oyaaa oaranga virangae
injuha a limunyumba
mshairi alimunyumba

In the whole world
Aluta continua
aluta continua

Juba-man-o'-war

That old tall thin bent black man at Totto Chan
in South Sudan
The ancient Jubaman of many wars
at a Children's center cooks so gentle
his image refuses to leave my mind
just like old and
lonely men I saw in our villages
and other cities

When Jubaman sat outside to rest after work
you could hear the tide of his memories
rise and fall, fall and rise, fall
telling to you long, long silent stories
quietly spreading around him
And a loneliness of knowing wrapped him

Old men, war veterans now
in tattered old shoes
To habari* they answer msuri*
Njema* has never been their sophistication
And sometimes they stare at you
with an open mouthed jambooooh*!
So the old man at Totto Chan
he will only say tamam*
and peace greeting smile
but I know
I know he still speaks
to the war
stupefied

His pelvic bones at the back became like two guns
covered thinly by a T-shirt that reads
Pax in terra, pax in coelo
Peace on earth, peace in the heavens
paix sur le terre
Peace on Earth
The Old man of Juba
His feet, long, long
are like two bigger guns that sound like thunder
two limbs whose toes have fired much
and not an extra grain of weight
splendorous texture and height

I wonder does he remember any traditional war stories?
He watches like one who knows modern survival techniques
He listens to the blessing of the haunting wind
He knows that Dafur is in our bones
and says that is why
we weigh more
We are heavy people
difficult

Kenya stares in Rwanda's eyes
This old man, like the old man of Nairobi
sits beside a kei-apple fence in town
its fruits are nowhere close to Adam's
neither the ones in your markets fair

In the City in the Sun
it is at Jevanjee where an old man
sits talking to himself
greening his roots

Like the old man in the streets of London
and gentle in a Viennese park so dazed
in Spring

In Juba the old man is transported
in a heat we could slice
Earth burns
Air burns
Wind burns
Wealth burnt
But under a thick arch held and formed
by two well kept bushes
he tells his story again
to the sun
It roasts it

He turns it to
the wind
it burns it
He is a cook

He waits for the moon
and the rain
to fall from
the finger of Garang blessing
ancestors demanding their continent
They are furious

Juba, March 2009

Totto Chan is the name of a center for children where the poet witnessed two boy soldiers and a girl soldier return.

Toto means "child" in Kiswahili.

Habari is a greeting in Kiswahili, which means "Any news?".

Mzuri is sometimes an answer and means "good" in Kiswahili, but here it is written as in the dialect of the humble and poor who have no use for sophisticated language.

Njema is seen as the classy way of saying "good"

Jambo could be translated as "Is there any issue worth noting?" It was the greeting of the colonizer in Kiswahili.

Tamam in answer to a greeting in Arabic and means "fine", timamu is Kiswahili for stable or prepared

I am your seed, Mother

We are always together
Wherever the dry wheels of life take me
wherever the oiled circles of life move me
When I cannot say my name
we are together
When someone winks at me and smiles
When a hand stretches to a horizon
May it be your palm like once it was your womb
When faces are weary and hearts fail Mother
When children and old men cry in women's hands
May yours like a gentle moonrise caress
pamper us caring

In the silence of the togetherness of the
snow that falls and hugs leaves
In the un-sensed warmth of thoughts
incubated in my skin the sun
In the mind that melts and loves and
knows – we embrace
We are always together and you hold
and adore my feelings ☺ heart in mind

In the thought that hugs all minds
In the weight of words unformulated
yearning
Unwritten, unheld, unloved
You are there
Beloved

11.10.2011

FLYING

Word

Eating word from the end
is the mirror light
Your word caresses my soul
Something is taking me
When I receive this gift
it blows me to where music is being
I want to stay there
a place where we are all
creating

Love steals in gently like rays from far away
And I have got to call them names now
This is not a soporific evening of tunes

Silence cut me
Silence blew me up
Silence drew me
And then I
Silence made me
With its notes
Word
Jesus you were not always bread
we heard you and others before

I dance to this new dawn of mind
LovE Evol
Mirror
Effect

Flight

On her funeral
she came flying in song
through
that open door
invisible to all
except the hinges
that smiled instead of creaking
They bent a little to sing
and the wind that she was
blew in
gently at first

Oh, so gently
and then all at once
the darkness fell and rolled
Curtain rise for the dead
For Whitney Houston
burial
you remember
A flight so high

And, I... I... I...

For she sang the sky clearly springing
wringing her pain in words
and the world shot through her
injections of
doubt, deep hurt no light
pain and more doubt
so deep

It is in the darkness of a such departure
we get to know how strongly
stars kiss light
how often in nightly clad
their life of strain is unknown
I toast
To Dolly Parton your part is high and on
Miley Cyrus open this door
This other one died
on stage as was her desire
but Makeba buried her daughter
in untold lonely
stand
All her beloved asleep like apostles
Miriam Makeba
rise again with healing
Voice
to voice
singing again Whitney
to the soul of the world
And I iiiiii
iiii will always...
love you...
Dancing soul reflect -
Pata pata is the name of the dance
I feel pata pata pata

If I could

If I could
Mother
I would lift the curtain
that makes my dreams
a performance my audience
too far to hear
my own voice
broken to touch
too lost to bear me
except in your soul

If I could
Mother
I would change the phone
so it brings me to you
and the computer
so it would allow me
bi-locational power if for a minute
just to touch your skin
in this moment of exile

To see
to see your eyes move and
hear you speak again
telling me in my Ma Tongue
that nothing is too much
I would kiss you again

Perhaps we would even laugh
if you smiled as your tongue went

gũtirĩ ũndũ njogu!
Uuu
You are here!

Indeed
there is nothing elephant

If I could, Mother,
the world would be one
languaged
in understanding
Our country would be revered
we would all be fighting for justice
without causing some to flee
We would all be happy
rescuing the many abused
Healing mental wounds

But for now, Mother
I cannot
I have to hide
even from your breast
Reading Solzhenitsyn
on cold pavements river frozen
I have to be happier
learning that in life
a sister can be a stranger
and a new face the best brother

Safer on this safari
even if safety today
is a holy illusion

so for you too
Mother
I light a candle daily
Our land is safe no more
I weave a halo
I melt the moment of our meeting
I meet from far the moment our eyes will
take
eat together
this broken sign
Our sacrament
of life

Leaving Juba

Wave a little *Kwaheri**
airport trepidations
Even blanketed in heat
still here liquids matter
you cannot sip a little as you fly
the flies

How to make expeditions
with only solid matters
how to?
Waters must connect us
rain makes us one
but I leave Juba in Sudan

How to break with song
that moves from the waves
from the land of Garang**
one with the Nile
leave?

How to?

Longing, loving, braving
enjoy a little more heat
Here in this is immense burner
How to
without your mind caving in
be grateful for this heat
in the winter of your heart?

How to
believe in more poetic roads
verse
as it speaks to breathe Jubaland
moves to believe in herstory
How to see
two lands shake hands out of the cities
of our one land
bringing tides rural
where we are still one
How to?

March 2009

* Kwaheri is goodbye and literally "with blessing' in Kiswahili.
** Dr. John Garang is a military man who fought in the forest and captured power in Sudan. He died in a plane crash on mountains on his way from a meeting with the Ugandan President. He had a doctorate in agriculture.

Diplomatic happy hour

All here have taken vitamins
and eat well in Europe
with the EU locals who eat us too
we are community abroad
The sun is not dry in me
I see
It is written on their faces
with mascara, rouge
lipstick and powders
that gently rub in there
The sun is roasted in me
black
They came to eat minerals
To show off everything
And then sleep very hard
making love not war they are content
The memory is not lost on us
long time ago in the bushes
but now we are they

They supplement their lives
dreams, skins
and hair and nails
and breasts and stomachs
and shoulders and legs
broken inside
clothes of fashion too are bandages
souls toil within thin skin
Here full people stuffed with food
My soul is outside my skin

Perfumes in the air kiss
and hiss at one another
nothing is pure or was
Huge on Hugo Boss on
Straws of Khan's Skin
hit on and mix
stink money
For Binti al Sudan
taken dignity from the poor
there is no voice, no comfort
don't speak dissidence
there are tablets to keep you cool
Motherlands raped beyond gender
They eke the sun in us
Many have taken Cod Liver Oil
to make sure the bones
stay strong and the mood don't swing
normal without the sun
coffee is a must black being
best
I wanted to love you but you
saw only skin
and bones
my words you cast off
like stitches
leaving one

Here creams are more expensive
than Mary's ointment
find them in the solarium
seeking out the sun

But Mary herself disappeared
her long hair hidden in a gun
of Amina's man

In the sauna they are sweating
The Isca riot stands in the corner gawking
Which of them can he sell?
They have all eaten well and dream deep
Slavery did not leave my eyes
I sleep in the gutter and see the stars

In winter we suck warmth from everything
girls from far lands are roasted
As the world keeps burning our lives
we need one more
sign of contradiction:
Continent worst hit by climate change
is Afrika
keep a HAT for
Happy Ambassadorial Times!

Sunrise for Roma

Today the sun rises warm
defies the winter shivers
It dawns for me I know
but
first for the Roma who sits
on ice outside Rema Supermarket for seasons
on cartons and cloths and smiles
and a cajoling
'Good morning!' and a 'Thank you! Please!'
That not one of the vitamin takers
remember to say

But the Roma nods into a cup of
cartoned sorrow outside Rema
Nodded and smiled to the teeth
held together without vitamin D
supplements are blankets of the rich

She sits there now, stills the moon
Teeth braced by ice in Oslo
the freeze of the drink of life without smiles
and still she sings the notes of her song
this life of chains of pain embraces the world

And in the evening the music of the Roma was stolen
and sold
taken by the big booming sounds in the
DansHus as dancers skate and fly off
snowflakes without a cinderella stroke

In there the fashion - able stole my gipsy skirt
Food for tasting but not eating
Now this type, and now the other
tasting and testing and crunching each bite
We buy more to add to what is at home
tomorrow fashionistas have a new brand
But
The Roma has drowned in shallow Akerselva, rolling
Like the dancers he has gone into a trance of
glory in hunger and dreams of his hope in humanity
Did he need any ashes on his head
to make us sorry for our sins?
What then do our dance steps in the air
matter?

I count my ribs

This is the one they say Adam gave me
And that it makes the whole of me
It is broken and made into dust by Adama
Broken ribs by Adama, his type, Adamu, his uncle
and blood, aaaa, Adamu!
and his kin of blood, including my brother
Government bullets rip many chests

The rib you see below
it is
broken by fathers at war
All these ones are sewn by sisters
chiseled, drilled and nailed by others
chasing others
and…

the ribs all over my
body in my heart
and soul broken by
rape
It is my toes that hold my life
I run when I walk

Pen in my wings whispered to by brain
I still fly in my dust when I write
and even sing: we must overcome!
No tũkahotana! Notũkahotana!
Victory is not a choice
We have to define our own
Surmounting

No tūkahotana!
Proudly survived

Allah Akhbar

I know you my friend
Thank you for your dreams always of sweet
Lords to deliver us from ourselves
good heavens who is washing any feet now?
The pebbles in the river scrub them

At night news breaking till NRK shuddered
I heard that the Christ arrived with a whip and
backsides are red and painful for those
there who listened to him and heard

He was shouting *Allahu Akhbar! Allah Akhbar!*

I heard that only a black madonna undressed
and Mary Magdalena were walking beside him
all the others
dancers and choreographers
audience and caretakers
spilt his wine which he made in Cana
There is no wedding in Oslo, no wedding
He and
his new friends will find other fjorded seas
But
tomorrow we shall dress for a baptism
for 'dorp' and beg the Roma for a drop of water
To cool our burning tongues and breaths of song and dance
Lazarus' name is preserved
We are so right
A diva roams the forests singing to rivers
At first she run away when she heard this story and now

she wears a laurel and waits for the rays of the sun
and hears a muezzin calling out again
and Jesus Issa answers him in reply
Allahu Akbar, Allahu Akbar
Chiming bells
ahhha
bells ringing in hours
the Muezzin will be back early
Allaaaaah Akbar! Allaaaaaah Akbar!

Beauty

I think of you beauty that
brings me near
I connect and you are faraway
I disconnect and ask you to help me
Help me
listen to myself
to the world keenly from the start
Help me listen
so I may speak
Listen so my passionate heart
is not finished
consumed
in the moment of the spectacle
when it burns your beauty

High

It will not be one step
after the other
It will not be any steps
You know my wings are here

I will not be breathless then
Your chains will turn to rust
the tips of my toes will be sailing
I will smile and see your cells so distant

I will not need to ask for my Love
He will be there
She will be there
in an endless embrace we shall sing
Hum if we like
and no need of pain again
I taste this on my tongue
hmmm
High

Stereo plays

I fear your type is permanent
That you look at a river and see
only ducks sitting yet all birds
here are flying in reflection see the sky
You look at a dark rock and say
they are all of the same color

You saw animals on all fours
and declared all are equal and
always on fours including millipedes
the fish that swim and
we had to tell you about snakes
that crawl hiding poison and bite
a body to kill
You said that soul turns into fire
burning
I then saw you look at an evergreen tree
and your silent words bore the winter
all trees evergreen you say are ever the same
that all trees are tall and straight and
you have not seen
the baobab and the acacia

I hear you say that only the dark skinned do not go
to watch plays and enjoy theater
in a city where two spots claim culture
I do need a sigh now

People stare at machines
and destroy everything else I prefer to be

I want to listen more to life
not forever be stiff
Stereotype necklace
burns
deep like chains on fire
Heavy
it scorches beyond
but seriously
how else do you roast spirits
except in alcohol?

Wash me

Silent light so bright and dark
came in, invading me
peeling off heaviness
felt it melt away
silent soft light
of music
I felt it make a way
deep in my ringing soul meditating
Birth, rebirth

Peals of laughter
swang open my being
How softly my wings
there can be no door
for an open soul embracing
not disengaging–

light hiding
darkness splitting
in the creases
and watering
the crises of life
to a blooming green
in your notes
full of composed
creativity

You got the best part
of me feeling

no hypocrisy
Rage rises endless
Silent light so bright and dark is on

RAGE

So Betrayed

2011 Nov 18

When the sands of time
into my face flew
They parted ways in a thousand particles
that split my blood into several voices of power
The winds blew my wings into a raging storm
I wrested a knife from the pharaoh's hand

The waves should not wash your feet in music
Tell your feet now
that all must run faster to knock at doors
My sister lies on the island bleeding
can we sleep tonight?
A baby girl cries mutilated, small eyes searching she dies
I am raging, seeking, trying
I am a wave hugging shores
Mining angered peace

My mother escaped death as I came through a slit
Insanity is not maiden I want all my sisters back
Back whole and complete undo traditional ways
You stand and wait for reason and diplomacy am gone
All alphabets I return to Alpha all stars to before creation
This G spot garden is ours

Swooping and surveying the islands of the pain of mutilation
I say again that my sister is lying on the island, on desert
sands alone
sighing and bleeding, weeping for centuries with her Ph. Ds
Turn all the world's bright fabrics into handkerchiefs

She turned on her lights who dares switch them off?

Light up Tahrir Square at midday's night again
Invisible freedom serve me not, give body voice to my sisters
My bare feet shackled take the knife from the doctor's hand
Light up all parks today and let all women be truly free

Throw that knife, deep into the pit
Come back tomorrow to tell me about roots

There is no cotton if she dies there there is no silk upon your breast!
Around your neck there are no pearls if she dies there
On your wrist the watches of time scream
amulets are broken
The ankle chains break, take off your tie, high heels and run
No celebration in parliaments
my sister lies on an island bleeding

To say the iron bar lies in religion is certain error
The truth of a million years woman born to fly
Woman born gorgeous, clean and complete
Magnificence we turn into indecent dignity stolen
Trampled and crumpled
a demented elephant would be kinder

My Sister is on the island and she bleeds many colors
The sword came parting the ear the agony in the sea
The lip and skin and tenderness shredding heart
soft parts of life shedding blood that she must bleed again

An hawk can swoop up its own to safety with talons

Why are you waiting for the strong tide to wash her?
My sister is on the island still bleeding pint gallons
Why are your limbs limp and swiftness boxed in iron books?
Chains break now, break, break, break,
stand up and voice

A million years have endured pain and my sister still lies on
the island
Bled all colors, lips tightened, she cannot scream
I cannot sit here and hear another lamentation
Record this as dead history inside that pyramid
If this is not her promised flower
all her story turn to naught

If I have no eyes send me an eagle
Shake fake scrolls of belief when they
mislead you
Let me redeem the wisdom of the owl
that faith would cover in error
In time am a sparrow you
cannot break this arrow
Thousands of years I pierce
like a ray cutting against the grain of sand
To find organs in desert lands lying
Then let woman's ululation be mute
We are womanity let impunity cease
Reclaiming humanity still crying on the island

All perfume gathered in bottles yank out
All soaps laden with fragrances shed innocence
Oh incense rise not, burn not tonight in the cathedrals
tonight

All frankincense in homes gather back into your sticks
Light a fire with myrrh and flame it out

Stop that train and make the rain wash the sky of pain
The horizons of centuries covered with earth blood
Make 7 billion and 20 candles for all girls born today
Creative dynamic let trumpets blast till the top
Take my pencil and gather its voice too, snap!
Now
take my chest and open it to find my heart and read it
Take my life and sip it because
my sister still lies bleeding on the island
I say to you, yesterday was study, today is action
My sister's body, must be free: One word: free
Wash her feet, the skies and the island and
my sister set freeee, set her freeee!
friiiiiiii riiiiriiii frii friiiiiri! frii riririririr ah!
Break free of traditions that in radiation kill
You say this is looking down on our land
I have looked up for so long
I now look in me
I must work on this island of blood
till sunrise

Fresh

Like a big drop
of water round
Universes
reflect the sky
take the color of
the moon

Look at it rolling
on a big strong
green leaf of life
A drop of water -
Silent all horizons here are

Once upon a time
you were a drop rolling
taking planets
Mars all red in your mother's womb
Shredding and readying
until you embedded
and you are still rolling
Our universes spread in books
Our love
Whole you are

Never seen my body

One tress after the other
my kinky hair
Beauty in black managed by fingers
taking soul from root to head and heart
Look
I have seen my image before many mirrors
never seen my body and never will
Why all this fuss about hair?

A glance is not enough
another way is within insight
Not in the eyes but in my whole
A collection of my oneness a sure gift
so many things inside
If I forgot I am one would I be two?

The winds come gently stealing
through very hot air and they take
They take the little moisture left
and show that they brought
calm relief their virginity stolen
Look
I have never seen my body
We have never seen what we saw
Who knows what we know?

Gu'nai

Gu'nai my sweet Mum
across the oceans in another horizon
Waking up two hours before me to
remember me, to encourage me
Gu'nai, Good Mum
Good night

Gu'nai I told her with a phone message
read to her by the iris of my eye
that stays there with her
And to make it personal
and make her laugh
remind her I am her pupil keen
and still dashing
in her eye with no saying goodbye

I tell her again "guuu...na aiii" how we used
to say it in family language
There are precious moments
of innocence
that become pure heaven
all senses in one

Good night my sweet Mum
I hear your laughter
like lightning it reached me before
the thunder of the telephone
raged so what
Good night my most loved sweet Mum
I feel your touch

One day I will hop on a craft running to meet you
I hear your voice
Good night sweet Mum
you make me laugh too
We shall sleep in your laughter and endless love
taste and kiss your eyes again
they have seen pain in their gentleness

Refuge

If you had not given me refuge
I would have found it impossible
to start again with confidence
like a spider, pulling its own thread
to make a web, spinning its castle
no matter how delicate

I had lost the illusion you see
and the most difficult thing
is to restart that part in your soul
that believes it can
That part they try to kill
but will never succeed

I know there is no haven
Dar es salaam too had a bomb
I know the world is restless
but your caress has kept me
dressed in my robe of sanity
for a while
yea tho pain drips raging
it returns strength in my sackcloth

Pain has kept my soul alive to me
so it can feel another's hurt
It has kept me alive to all
so we can celebrate a new year
from hut to hut
and heart
Let there be a stir for

the world's
New Year

A Saturday sunrise

In the horizon
an old church spire
pierces the quiet morning
industrial smoke rises too

I am watching actual reflections early
The open sky has come to meet us
here dawn is at 9.30am
your nights are long
darkness fell at 3 in the afternoon yesterday
a Friday

Something has stilled the
blackened twigs of trees
this windless Saturday morning
they do not swing like church bells
the snow lies quietly melting
The temperature is one above zero
I hope it will rise higher tomorrow

But the sky is open and
seeing light clouds shot with orange
I feel warm in my heart
this splintering silence renews me
gives me strength

To mock the lack of movement
a white crow has cut a cross
a broken horizon
and passed to meet sparrows

in a Victory formation
Their message in a morning
after firecracker outburst
is difficult to footnote below

The sparrows have come thrice as if to say
soon you will see
the victory rising in your dawn
I raise my cup and take a gulp
The church spire now bathes in solace
in noon light high
it is three degrees

I know we are near, one year has ended
another has begun, with so much color it has landed
someone had captured us, grey doves in their hands
and now our beaks break free in speech

A long journey, begins with a desire
Mine is so strong why am I still here?
When the first step is taken
there is no turning back
If you turn then it was a short walk you took
We all must be free to see change
unfolding slowly in a pod

This moment is my gift, I will move it, so it won't wilt
until I put it to you in golden silt
and without a doubt you will see
it was worth every risk
The sun rises with a promise to rise again
broken horizons they maybe but

warmth returns

Christiania home
Eve of 2011

Joy has been calling me
making me know that I must
now always be standing on top
of my little mountain
That in every situation
I can only think of winning

You lit many candles there last night
some watched in deep prayer
Young eyes moved in to hold tight
to your faith in humanity making humanity
weaving it now like a rope

I will remember all the prayers
For Russia and for South Africa
For an Ivory Coast of peace
A healed Kenya after 2007
In Nigeria a new election
the struggle for Afrika persists
prayer for religions that hold peace as roots
yearning for places and cities to work out
The Middle East is in my chest

Working for peace behind the scenes
not making news but taking every wound
and trying to prevent another rush of hot blood
I know my moments flood with doubts
when no one knows how many die
You have a clean bandage for my pain

with it I can wipe my tears of blood in words

There is a mosque in your courtyard
I took off my shoes to peep there
Little ones take refuge here in peace
not every mind is glad
See how
their names are soiled by
fundamental lists
Their souls want living peace
their faces are crying with fear
outrageous

There is a temple in your
Christiania home and prayer peace rises there
like incense
Bhuddist temples homes of surgery too
You have experts in Tai chi
Discipline the world and teach it
urgency
But this first candle is for my son
making courageous turns in your land
where variety still invites rejection
Dark skins here change name for success
Maybe Olso for Christiania
and again Kristiania to Oslo
was a telling change
But joy has been calling me
in every situation to only think
of winning

Nautical smiles

We have to be there
there in the late autumn
when the mist rolls
We have to be there
when it lifts in steam

We shall be in Torcello
and we have been in Venice
without the merchants of interest
rates
just us
Looking beyond horizons
our smiles breaking over the water
and spreading out for miles
we find a silent haunt

The footstep of an old man on the sea
whispering waves of water hemming ways
on Torcello island far away and foaming on the
hem of her skirt like filigree soft lace reminds me of you

and you Indian Ocean foam dancing gently round my toes
seas calm and seasons too for a while, look
Listen
Sing me a lullaby before the gathering storm
Let us write longer poems on our Kangas
that sometimes we were glad and happy
Kissed
loved and free even if we still hid tears in our beads

Even if we had to squeeze
our souls into words
to live

Nairobi soils

Nairobi soils and pavements
are crumbling in our hands, see
Women have always cultivated
land and freedom, words and sense

Now
our faces are wrinkling in the sun, see
Women had wanted to bathe in freedom and justice
Our hands are skinless in labor, see
Our breaths hot and cold rise, see
We evaporate in the shimmer of the mirage

Our dreams are waking in the heat, look
Our drums are playing in the mud, hear
Our voices are… broken once, twice, thrice, infinity
And then we rise like a wave in the ocean
With our hands in our soils and we begin again
The place of cool waters
the place of cool waters indeed?
Nairobi, our souls and soils in Kenya and the villages
We turn again
and now our hands are tired women
our legs, eyes, ears, throats
and hands and yes, skin and bottoms
And we are stripping naked again for
Freedom, this struggle is forever
The pavements are screaming in the air
and hair is flying in our eyes and blinded
you cry that women
that women

       that women
         what?
　Place of cool waters
　Place of cool waters
        indeed

Bouquet

I have just unwrapped
the paper
and cut the stems obliquely
something another thought Afrika
does not know how to do
There is a list
of what an Afrikan knows in the do-dictionary
And you, Afrika, they say
have never been that
way flowery
you only grow flowers for export
and I add
flowers yes and
all your blood groups to the world

I fought this battle in words in the 90s
But no then people learned Afrika is a country
Spanish Sol said poor people
could not handle the trade of flowers
with their hands
could not hold roses kindly enough
if they were not working for the elite
who have the smoother hands, you know
to know how to hold and cut a stem

As if the peasant is not our God on the
mountains and hills dying in rivers
Why is this alive this century?

Creamy red centered

red, red roses they gave me
at Lambeseter in Norway
for connecting with Kibera in skies of skype
I will keep my roses until they dry out
and take the sap back with me to Afrika
How much blood has dried since?
and write a story the rose you wear cost a miscarriage
you wondered why the fragrance thinned?

I will lay another bouquet of deep red roses
on your carpet and you will see them smile
when you come back and unwrap life
as I sing you and see our healing land
As I sing you in the moonlight of my soil
heart, blood, purply ways of life brightening
with flowers of freedom and reason

I will place your plant in a pot
to remember this day
Will take one big cactus and
I will touch
the thorns as if they are kisses
on my happy gentle cheek so loved
and tell them stories which flowers only tell flowers
for they are the bones of soldiers dead fighting in desert
lands drinking alien waters for their country and stepping
tell them to stop stepping hard the country is not their groins
though underpants they may wear in the colors of aggressive
flags
You know no distance between things so
with your lips please dry my tears that now pour

So I am the flower conceived
now and I thank
I will take two flowers
old and dry bouquets home
On that day you and I will sing
One for Kibera and one for why
we leave so we can stay

You and I will cut hope
and eat in peace
When my motherland's hand stretches
kindly towards mine – ours

Morning unfolds for some

This is a spectacular morning
Unfolding last face of December disappearing
inside it wrinkles the face of winter
Here in Oslo the sunshine is promising
To abandon the south and return to us
laden with Vitamin D, we smile
we long for it
Here the miller is a tablet

I was about to run out the sky is so clear
True of this day of December the feeling
is an aged strung one awaiting rejuvenation
with the kiss of the tender and new baby
that comes at midnight with lights and shrills and
Joy everywhere including my village where
no silent night, for the women scream

It is Xmas, the X
the season for cutting
and beating women anywhere
Eat, drink and drive
for tomorrow we lie

to the children
Here like all places I have been this time is alive
Old and New in the same breath so voiced:
Happy New Year, Godnyttår, Feliz año Nuevo, Skaål!
Cheers! Afya! Hongera! Shabash! Bashhhh!
Here
Likestilling is a new alcohol

Social equality
even in drinks we count same glasses
Everyone is drinking øl, beer and more
finer qualities up there

And more and more

I search for renewal of mind
In the morning, I take my spoonful of
Møllers Tran for these bones and dry skin
nobody who drank remembers
dry and shrink in the wetness of drink
let's toast to reflections

For those up late Fr Xmas has vanished
Here the miller, møller in Norwegian
Visits us every day instead of the sun
Bringing sunshine for us to swallow in a tablet
So I watch daily for New Year in a special way

A year like there has never been
marked with
no headlines of violence
I am groping in the dark

I cannot count his ribs

His ribcage is like that of a giant pumpkin
bone so well covered
rounded over every corner
Who says he gives me a rib
I am not allowed to count the ribs of my man
you would say he has none on those hard muscles used to
pumping

He is a heavy burden above me
He counts his property like this:
Money is loaded on degrees, wives, cars,
girls, suits, ties, offices
State meetings drinks worth a family's monthly budget
he pours in drinks for friends in an hour
Absinth, Bourbon, Castle Lager, Dry Gin
Grappa, Limoncello
Uozo, Raki, Captain Morgan, Baileys
Sweet wine red and white, dry and wet
Champagne so very often
Tusker, Muratina, Waragi for hard weekends
and happy evenings Tequila and Amarulla
under the shade after a swim
before after inviting to Casa del Diablo
A massage was first
gym for muscle and Spa too to spy
I forgot Scotch and Irish Whiskies, Italian
and French ways overdone

The list is endless
from State House to the shanties

It includes goats and cattle
land and deals in diamonds
dirty pebbles along the way for models should be dropped
for her to see and admire
Maybe just learn their names
Dirty rubble from some beaches unknown
in a camera country
where heat of stone warms long bones
I know

I am not allowed to look at his ribs
when he clicks the cufflinks
of his shirt and I polish his shoes
At such times when he speaks with
things filling his ears to a small phone
shaped like another wife
His white vest fits well I see
when it gets sweaty and dusty
it is mine as are all his underwear
but he beats me if he sees mine

What those little waters he splashes on are I know
and I can read Old Spice
before on his neck he knots a tie
to keep the heat of the sun from touching
his apple
so well shone
I will scorch it the next time he tells me
the rubbish he said in Bunge

I studied when the sun shone
When the harvest was done

I got a degree but he
said that literary type is for women
who wear kangas
all day long calling me a soft head
and now he has an MBA written on
Mercedes Benz Africa big back woman
I know his underbelly
Certificates are for money not for prince apples
He removed the homegirl's kanga
and pulling on without socks
even you
his ribs roasting how to count them ever
he lit another fire and introduced her to
my children as his next wife
to be housed in Kayole
There is already a little one in the young womb
and he thinks I will sit here and cry?

I shall uproot this pumpkin in the old homestead
and am not ashamed Okot
There are so many things
we must part ways
How shall earth bear this and the rocks of Maragoli?
How shameless Ocol you spit at Kit Mikayi
you the
modern one
This is not lipstick or
roasted hair that we can take off
This is it

Do I have to reason with you that Lawino
must always pretend to know Akinyi

is coming to help grow your seeds when what you bring is
death
You take here and take there
like a buffalo that is never satisfied
Times having changed you drive on as if you are blind?
You keep your head straight direct to your mistresses
I tell you it is not the constitution that will rule out polygamy
but I
that will
by my way and hand
a new law write
You were spared then
but now I pull by the roots
If you resist
I take yours first, your third leg until your boots fly off
These things done behind our backs are killers
Polygamy -when it was- was an open space
Everyone who married who was known in the dance
Kit Mikayi's shrine is defiled

Now you say that is a lie
and you take with you all power
and also all the land
the voices of our nation you inherit
Who shall I marry then, who shall I marry Ocol?
I want to uproot more than a pumpkin Ocol I want to...
I am going to uproot this pumpkin of your oppression
This pumpkin oh
I must
take it by its very roots
It is a male type that never bears fruit and will never
It kills a continental globe now listen out there

His power makes me a stranger to my own home
He does not know what it is to be a mother refugee anywhere
in the world
What it is to be the son of no woman like he pretends to be
Highland pumpkin you are not a king
Like the lowland one I will get you down
until you bear fruit
I will uproot the pumpkin in your highlands
and all its seeds scatter further into land
that was called barren and it will grow and cover us
The homestead is gone and the churches are ruined

Litanies are sung by African ancestors your ribs are not close
to mine
Come and show me one Eva Mumbi you ever did make
You unmake them
and you grow like a pumpkin that
throttles with tendrils instead
of being soft and mellow to mash and eat

I will count my own ribs, my children's and let yours go the
way
of those who remove kangas from innocent girls' waists,

Chira!
Chira! Chiiira, Chiira! Chiraaaa!
Kungu Kit Mikayi, Kungu Kit Mikayi
Kungu Kit!
A curse from my nakedness!

Fragrances

I smell the fragrance of your skin
and know how it was when it touched mine
I feel the traces of your life around me
in fragrances
Your warmth and dreams falling from your lips

I see in your eye mirror held before me
I move to catch your breath
So that we breathe life
And then blowing our breaths on the mirror
shine it more and more
so that we see each other
shining
Sparkling and
joyful in soul!

Warrant of arrest

Raging
I will be in your arms
You are my warrant of arrest
I will love you
With my warrant of arrest
I will sing to you
With my warrant of arrest
I will eat with you
With my warrant of arrest
I have been breathing
With my warrant of arrest
I shall dance and shout
With my warrant of arrest
Dance truth to your churches
With my warrant of arrest
Dash patriarchy
With my warrant of arrest

You give it to me
Because I sang freedom
Well may it sing yours too
because I said corruption is death
there are many types of dying
and sins

Dafur genocide is haram, Dafur injustice is haram
Haram terror, haram all terror
it is deicide
Haram rape and haram handcuffs
Torture is haram

Piracy haram
Your injustice so old haram, haram
haram, haram
Salaams?

Well may your soul hear that again
because you know I would not rest
Well now am ready for the test
Let's strip naked your warrant of arrest
Am back to nurture the law
of freedom in every way
With my warrant of arrest
and in freedom create unceasing
I will love you
I love you
with my warrant
of arrest
on my chest
You
Salaam

www.ingramcontent.com/pod-product-compliance
Lightning Source LLC
Chambersburg PA
CBHW021936160426
43195CB00011B/1110